Riverside Poets Anthology

Riverside Poets Anthology

Volume 21
New York, New York
2021

Executive Editor	Norma Levy
Editors	Philip De Pinto, Terry Edmonds, Art Gatti, Mara Levine, Anthony Moscini, Peggy Murphy, Paul Oratofsky, Kristin Robie, Fred Simpson, David M. Williams
Production Editor	Lora Wanta
Cover Photo by	Roxanne Hoffman
Special thanks to…	Anthony Moscini for leading the Riverside Poetry Workshop, the source of these poems The New York Public Library and the Riverside Branch staff for providing a home to the Riverside Poets for many years Those whose encouragement and support helped to make this book possible

Riverside Poets
c/o Norma Levy
142 West End Ave Apt 27L
New York, NY 10023
nlevynyc@aol.com
riversidepoetrygroup@gmail.com

ISBN: 9798426434585

To the victims of Covid-19
and good friends lost

And a special tribute to:

Marcia Edelman-Ostwind
June 22, 1937 – May 1, 2021

Cece Wasserman
November 19, 1937 – May 1, 2020

Ode to us

The size of small is hard to
tell   The number of pin points
on an angel's head can't be known

None are sure how small small is

We might say there are no little poetry
groups   only tiny minds
thinking some poetry groups
are merely fragments

Stars seem minuscule
yet they're large   So it is with our
New York poets   Thought by some to
be tiny or unknown   Perhaps
remote   But like each star we're
bright   constant   and   increasingly
known   Perhaps everlasting

Anthony Moscini

Table of Contents

Riverside Poets Anthology

Epitaph

When they bury me
Let them play
Shubert's
Quintet in C
Let the honied melodies
Swell over me
and the warm embrace of cellos
tell how I loved music,
My violin, and you close to me
I will try to be
near to you if that can be
To watch my daughters
and their tall sons
range round the globe
Following after me
Bone of my own
Muscle and brain
Sagittarians called
To wander the world:
Think of me when
Schubert's Adagio sings in C

Transcending

Escher got it right.
Men step down and yet rise up,
the hand is drawn by the hand it draws
and a woman is poised
on her very own shoulders.

Without you and me this universe is simple,
run with the regularity of a prison.
Galaxies spin along stipulated arcs,
stars collapse at the specified hour,
crows u-turn south and monkeys rut on schedule.

But we, whom the cosmos shaped for a billion years
to fit this place, we know it failed.
For we can reshape,
reach an arm through the bars
and, Escher-like, pull ourselves out.

And while whales feeding on mackerel
are confined forever in the sea,
we climb the waves,

The High Life

Plenty of planes in flight
Tallest buildings in sight
Not many birds alight
That's because of the height
Of my windows.

One sees tops of trees
All green until the freeze
Then changing of the leaves
Browns, yellow, rust, one sees
In my windows.

In the morning sunrise
When warmth opens my eyes
Pretty pink in the skies
A rainbow in disguise
Through my windows.

In the evening lights flow
The moon has a halo
It's alive, with gusto
From the park, all below
My windows.

Covering up?

Why do I cover

My skin with cream?
My body with clothes?
My face with a mask?

What am I hiding?

Sadness with a smile
Aging with make-up
My fears with a drink.

Why do I do this?

To hide my feelings,
To battle boredom,
To create something.

When does it happen?

Morning, noon and night
In all my day dreams
When I am sleeping.

Who knows about this?

No one until now
Everyone elsewhere
Facebook, CNN

The Garden of One Another

One seed is planted, then another
One takes root, then another,
They know not of one another,

One new life in suckling soil, then another,
A stem leaps up, reaching, stretching—then another,
They know not of one another,

Leaves in growth seek one another,
A bud appears in blush of color, then another
Yet they know not of one another,

A bud in the birth of bloom, one then another,
Floral splendor, on a palette of promise, one then another
Alas, they know not of one another,

The serendipity of the bee, pollen one then another,
The birth of blooming in one another,
The exquisite joy of knowing one another.

Stroke by Stroke

A painting birthed by a biased brush,
Hyperbole, alienation and distain,
Leaves no space for the nuanced eye,
For strokes of understanding, acceptance, love,

The hour has arrived…
To lift a gentler brush,
Paint a palette of softer colors,
Embracing all manner of hues.
Framed in empathy and oneness.
A canvas unblemished by the warts of willfulness,
There is no paintable “other,”
There is only a portrait of “we.”

the sea claims

the sea claims the
seagulls' voices,
talking nonstop
while footprints lightly
touch sand marks.

walkers pass,
joggers run,
and the earth swells
with white capped
waves
against the rocks,
foam-edged masterpieces.

the steam of salt air,
pure, refreshing,
renews one's essence.

moving along to a new school

walking alone toward
the elementary school,
watching cars and storefronts closed,
passing houses, sleeping eyes,
round me stilled
into little known cries.
I can't hush,
I'm the new child in class.
I run and hide
inside my skin.
I walk so slowly,
no longer in a city of bustle
and noise.
I soon must learn the meaning
of whys.
I watch the others take
a seat while I try to
cross my feet.
why am I here?
so new it is,
new friends to meet.
I must survive
and seek my stride
let go of old
and stay alive.

Akeem

how proud I was
of Akeem
asking the Principal
if he could see me
about his stuttering

5th grade, 10 years old,
and so proud,
his stride
waltzing down the hall
commanding respect
from all students

but
so knowing the help
he needed
and wanted

then, how he
delved into relaxation
exercises, situations
created
and acted these out
with smoother
words and sentences
so they could
truly
find their place
and speak
his heart.

Don't Stop Here

in this
soon-will-be
a desert

by its
stubble grass
parched –
stark rocks
sharp

by that
apple
shriveled
pulp-dry
dust-blown
to the ground

by this tree
wind-bent
sapless
bark shredding
bitten by bug-crawl

You will
grow
no leaves

Walker

My walker walks with me
leads me along this city street
past shadows in an alleyway
that reach out and call
Come join us   we'll embrace you
here among these decrepit garbage cans
this filthy litter strewn about
full darkness at our alley's end

But my walker knows the score
knows the sidewalks
tells me   No no   that place is not for you
Wipe it from your mind

Slow though I seem to be
my walker has become a second self
going where I want to   need to
assuring me with every pokey step I take
toward the Fairway Market two blocks away
an ATM I always use
the All-Night-Deli on the corner

What's the hurry   have no fear   be patient
don't stop   don't stop
You'll get to wherever you're going
soon

In a Country Store

"Ay-yuh – a lot has happened in this town
since you were here.

Simon Low, the chicken farmer, took the five mangy hounds
he owned down to the garbage dump, buried them alive
six feet under   That was a year ago

Since then, our organist, Flora, over at St. Pauls, got blown to bits
when a whole load of TNT she had stashed below the choir loft
exploded. She – the church – gone.
Fuck God and Bach, she used to mutter all the time.

Then Tim Foy, editor of ABOUT TOWN,
got sent down the river for ten years
because they found him giving blow-jobs
to high school boys in his cellar,
and just last Sunday afternoon Miss Susan B.,
our librarian, hung herself with a curtain cord in her attic
all because of a salesman who came through
stayed for awhile,   went.
A failed romance,

the rumor was.

Ay-yuh – a lot has happened.
Today our own Edgetown Giants beat Cornville
by five home runs –
First win since Hector was a pup –
You here for the square dance?"

For Anita O'Day jazzbird born 1919 still livin' on vinyl (after songs sung by this jazzbird)

And her tears flowed like wine dear Anita
You lost your sugar in salt lake
City alreet Kick it! just a little bit
South of north carolina where you long

To be two for tea and what's that, you think
What is this thing hi-ho trailus boot
Whip and you, O'Day marathon dancer in the common
Wind who speaks for scat alreet and the tears

Flowed like wine Kick it! build it up, paint it
Nice and tear it down dear O'Day O night
I can't give you anything but thanks for the boogie
Ride sideways sidewise O skylark gotta be gettin'

bolero at the savoy

blues for Bojangles

and his tears…

The airline stewardess and the bee

Just before takeoff on *Jet Blue*
a frequent flier shouted *a bee* *a bee*
the airline stewardess moved back

I'll take care of it—

she cradled the bee in a tissue
opened the plane door opened the tissue
and let the bee fly

a sparrow cradled its little one over Bethesda Fountain
in Central Park

a butterfly floated back
in Guadalajara

a fish leaped from the Gulf off the strand of Yucatan

Canadian Geese rose from the stream in Massapequa Preserves
with the soughing of Autumnal winds

a lioness sought her cub in the rushes of Nigeria

an elephant in the Congo mourned the death of her mate
her howl thrashing the leaves

where the bee is still searching for the palm of the angel
that gave her another life…

At the end of the day…

At the end of the day   it is   the end of the day
as everyone seems to say   join the chorus of
the end of the day   from the bully pulpit   from the
bully   bully pulpit   bully for you   bully for me
for all   that's all we have to say   bully for bulls
bully for blues   in twos   or toos
it sounds so final   after zero to zeniththought
in the Casino of Thought   where   there is no thought

just a rolo-dex   of Exes and Ohs   aught to naught
boomers to zoomers   we all want to sound
Apoca-Cryptic   Apoca-Lipstick   like   like
weave   given this a lot of thought   zero to naught
sold and bought   fraught and wrought   cast iron
a cast of thousands   of thoughts   at the end   end of the day…

Carcass

Thoughts are birds in flight

If you're lucky
a thought will fly away
and leave you rooted where you are
enfolded in life's quiet stream

If not, that bird
will nest in your mind
and hatch a tangle of little thoughts
that pin you down

and prey on the mind's flesh
spew it out
till nothing is left

Rose, My Breath

Is there anything more delicious
than the scent of a rose
beaded by early morning dew?
If I could only
make myself tiny enough
I'd climb in
and let soft petals
enfold my skin

No matter if those petals should fade
I'd simply leap into another
and – like a butterfly –
flit from one blossom to the next
perfume of the rose, my breath

When all the roses are gone
when all the leaves have dropped to earth
before the first frost comes
I'll burrow below ground
lie dormant among roots
a blanket of snow for warmth
and wait until June
living as roses do

Lay Me Down to Sleep

Take me in your arms
up the winding stair
to our room
and lay me down—
ever so gently

You may brush my brow
with your fingertip
if you'd like
place petals on my eyelids
or kiss my lips

Then, when you hear
my even breath in sleep,
sidle next to me
skin to skin
your legs entwined in mine
your body a blanket of blood-warmth

When I awake
I will feel your warm
hand on my thigh
your soft breath
quivering my cheek

and I will breathe easy
knowing you are still here…

The Bed

Because you slept in it
I kept it
After the fall
Headboard and all

The bed in which we rolled like dice
and tumbled in like weeds
The bed I watched you drift off
into reveries in
then rise like the morning star

I still have the original sheets
of our coital bliss – I always will
Other than this give or take the deluge or two
you wept like willows on blue pillows

I would say as well
I never venture to your side of the bed
and dare take comfort there
It seems I am too cowardly
both inwardly and outwardly

In doing so I fear
it would break its spell
the bed which I will never sell
at any price
or ditch in the street
It has for me
become too sweet
and endearing

Father What Joy

to be walking hand in hand
with your little boy
A hand which will never be
as little again

As will tend to grow
with the rest of the boy
big enough to hold
a little hand of its own

Father what Joy
to ferry such
all the way home
and squeeze down to the bone

And bold be the boy since grown
to brave a world without
a father's hand to hold

Only a wan and tiny stone
to clasp in his hand
to place over a larger
and darker stone
that heralds his grave

Fear Is The Moment

you sign on the ....line
The moment you're hired
to live this life till the moment you're retired
Fear is Superman minus a phone booth
who finds it difficult to change in a smart phone
Fear is not so sweet as a tooth
a broken necklace of teardrops to mop
No foam to skim off the top
It is beyond the brim – something grim
for you to keep – not borrow
Fear is no tent to fold or call to put on hold
It is every waking moment
And if you should be so lucky as to fall asleep
It is fear that watches over its investment – not an Angel

Fear is a wolf who has eaten all the sheep
you relied on to fall asleep
Fear is Cheetah lusting for Jane
dentistry before Novocain
Fear is dust confronted with a broom
An heirloom passed down generation to generation
Fear is the Prince seeing the slipper
fit on the wrong sister
Fear is the head of the pin seeing the size of the blister
Fear is Jack and Jill too beat on their feet to fetch a pail
Fear is being at a weight watcher's meet
while you have the weight of the world
on your shoulders as well as its monkey on your back
then told to get on the scale

Say His Name Too

(In memory of one-year- old Davell Gardner, Jr. who was killed by gunfire while sitting in his stroller on July 12, 2020, in his Bedford Stuyvesant (Bed-Stuy), Brooklyn, New York neighborhood during an outdoor barbecue)

We dance to
the inconsistent drumbeat of a
Brooklyn night in armor

Smoke hangs heavy as cement over a
half-lit, playground barbecue
There is no why in the alphabet of our intentions

A sudden stroke of fire cracks open strolling
slumber

Wonderstruck by thunder
there is no reason why
nestled in the bosom of July
a Bed-Stuy baby cries
no more

Turbulence

Cruising
fifteen hundred feet subzero
mid-flight above the arctic
ancient peaks of stone-edged passion
peek through clouds
half dressed in flimsy blankets of
windblown snow

The only sound
a slightly off-beat crackle of
watercolor blue ice melting
echoes of warming
extinction

A huddle of shivering penguins sit
shiva for the planet tonight

From every manmade bird's eye view
the rising sea murmurs:
Peace
be still no more

River Migrant

"No one leaves home unless home is the mouth of a shark"
- Warsan Shire, poet and activist

Swept off the land by invisible
hands of failing to grasp
what is a treasure
he pays a final mourning visit to the water's edge

Seduced by the wink and wave of soft river ripples
unprotected from falling
he boards a rotting bloated boat

The fitful journey begins

Turtleback stones like dead fish float
Trees are slowly turning into
bricks of shadows
His drowning eyes take flight in skies of
wild geese
  flying backwards

Strike of Seven

Real NY life cancelled, month after month
we hoot empathy, whistle oneness.
Pots bang, horns blow, and hands clap
to cheers heard across courtyard-chasms
as seven o'clock strikes with raucous zeal
and we howl from terraces and open windows.
Block on block of surly, bold survivors –
stir-crazed with masked confinement
hug and handshake denied by viral restraint
we bang and clap solidarity with fellow confines.
Restaurant-, theater- and tavern-deprived
we telegraph open-hearted empathy –
we're all with you sister, brother.
We're all still here.

Covid's Arc

Noah only had to float his boat
for forty days and nights
of drippy ho-hum, he and Mrs. Noah –
nothin' else to do back then
but roll around the hay they swiped
from kangaroos or maybe llamas
but then the sun returned
and all hooves danced on deck
so unlike now's catastrophe –
this viral deluge still falling endlessly
with month in and month out
of masked disaster.
What for do we deserve
this mean denial
I ask the heavens –
and could you please arrange
a smooth arc to recovery?

March Sun Kissed

This is a dismal season, morose
as love's slow demise –
gone, winter's crystalline glow.
The slow melt-back of sooty snow-time
mixed with a trifle of sunny enticement –
not enough heat to dig out
warm weather clothes, just earth
blowing you a few flirty kisses –
promises you her full-furnace passion
soon
if you don't succumb to despair first.

Elizabeth

they were deep square steps
leading from our second floor
you slowly bent each knee
breathing heavily under your weight;
at our landing you reached into
the faded silver milk box
lifted two damp white bottles
adding to already filled arms
your key tumbled the latch
I was at the door or turning
towards your voice
my mother greeted you with things to be done
I watched you snap your pocketbook clasp
over the key fastened to a frayed white string
you pushed the big plastic buttons on your
thin wool black coat, back through
the long stitched slits
your coat didn't give up
those heavy shoulders easily
as you slowly reached behind
tugging the snug sleeve free;
as I jumped up and down
you stretched your thick black arm to the wall
flattening your hand as anchor
I reached up locking my fingers together
suspended, laughing, swinging from your body

raindrops pool on roses and dazzle spider webs
but no raindrops ever touch so dearly
as I next to you

The Singer

slowly the stranger walked to the stage
leaving her walker near the bar
her girth covered in layers
a black turban set neatly on her head

the piano man knew first, the way
she offered her music in trust
she and the song already one, his generous
hands now, already promised to her

we knew one after the other
whoever heard the note…then the next
there was no wrapper, her sound peeled
free, our thirst drank rainwater

there was no shyness or coy femme
to bind or deny her leaping call
of lives stretching out or wailing
for another chance

when the M.C. introduced her
"she's had three strokes"
I wondered where she got the courage
to stand tall in the shadow of darkness

"careful you don't fall, careful you don't"…
or care fully when you can
our gratitude for her pounded from our palms
loving her and who we too might be

a warrior in prayer bearing beauty

I am loved by dreams
rapture in cigarette smoke
self-sung lullaby
a kiss stirs wings of a bird
grasping at leaves, she lets go

Lucky Is the Guy with Pfizer

Based on The Beatles', "Lucy in the Sky with Diamonds"

Imagine right now that you're down by the river
not six feet behind the ass of that guy. A sergeant just
told you, *Go onto the 5 line*. The guy looks incredibly high
Crystalline skylights, Javits-yellow and red, towering
over your head—Look for the guard who will show you
the path and she's gone

Ricky in the booth with needles/ Ricky in the booth with needles

Follow her down to a chair by a station where khaki-clad
people are there as your guide. Everyone smiles as you
drift through the hour, a time that quickly slides by
Newspapers tell you you're really quite lucky that
Covid will soon go away – Take fifteen minutes in chairs
six feet distant…and you're done

Ricky in the booth with needles/ Ricky in the booth with needles

Down escalators a million miles long, conductors angels today
Suddenly, quickly you've gone through the turnstile
your death fears have all gone away
Rubbing your arm at the 7 Train station where plastic wipe
raggers wash graffiti sides. Now you can be part of the
safe generation and put those damned masks all aside

Ricky in the booth with needles/ Ricky in the booth with needles
Ricky in the booth with needles….aaaahhh

Industry

Sputtering
street
lamp
alone

Moon of deserted
avenue and
grey-shut factory
wallness

blinking blind to the
pink smog
horizon
strip

Lone night bird
the only cloud
in the
concrete sky

Dust of
morning
hours
away

Wheels on Fire

I'm here on the Cross-County Parkway, ramming dark
with the nose of my car
I'm cutting the road and the Bronx in half
tires so hot that I'm smelling the tar

Yeah, I'm spurting along on the highway
the asphalt's a little unclear
I'm a rage and a roar on the pavement
while laughing and drinking ten beers

I'm here on the Cross-County Parkway
angels all clustered around
Ain't that me that hovers above me
with this heavenly horde I've found?

I'm here on the Cross-County Parkway
Like hell hounds the cars all zip by
Their horns are the trumpets that bear me
from the roadway clear up to the sky

I'm here on the Cross-County Parkway
I'm here and I'll always be here
So flash me a flash of your headlights
and listen…is that me you hear?

I'm here on the Cross-County Parkway
I'm here and I'll always be here

The Last Hurdle

I looked for you
everywhere

Behind buses
under stairwells
over bridges
even in ditches…

You were
nowhere

Time to go now
I must misplace you
outside these lingering thoughts
once and for all

Whatever it takes
to stand still…
with a lost vision
I can no longer recall.

Tamarind

a family of us grew
off Palm Beach Road
in background, not the botanical
a variety called Tropical

Hurricane Anna near the big lake
where it's rumored Osceola is buried
A purgatory of heat

weathered by our Spanish
English, and Portuguese ancestors
slips from the tongue

a mix between sunshine
or lemon-lime, but
orange

born between yellow
and red, if not dead
from the heat

only visible by light
only hindsight.

Black Friday

you come every year
appear as an ad or
sale flyer, you want me
to buy, or to try to stand in line

feel bought or sold, cower
to an institution or company
sad, rush after the push
and pull, deplete of energy

but I stand there, like chattel
indigent, bent on consumption
drink your prohibition. I know
do not need you, yet

I do follow through
to the counter, pay forward
storyboard my clutter, further
with the bric-a-brac

my lack is mind control
told, I sold myself
to the establishment
to the wealth management

then, I take it back
and say, I do not need
that.

Nonsensical during the pandemic

I just sit here. weight. a paper weight. I decided to use periods this time to stop. trying to judge me. trying to tell me I should capitalize. that becoming my horoscope is holding the fate of days in the astrology-stop. I did not attend paragraph New York; just could not. I just could not form anymore on this page, so I wait for you, to build something invisible in me; a tree top; maybe a trampoline the way the heart does in Spring, but the weather changes this time of year. The clear of snow yet remains a prediction. It's not skeptical; and the predictable is still in print. Trying to pay rent and compete for this modicum of fame. walking in transport with the rest of them; who have not broken through the academy. The glass walls that many do not see , but I see you in my fantasy; in my Zadie Smith moment. My power reading at night. Not interested in your discourse. Your distrust-stop. Not interested that you did not bother to find out-stop. This is not the end for me-not a rap star or claim of lyricism. This is a schism of the church, the borrowed white pants of winter-stop. It's the sign of the judgement. no government hand-outs in poetry. And she told me she spent money to be published, but she did not beat the pavement. but she did not beat the tom-toms of Langston Hughes. And they still disown me. This is motherless Brooklyn. This takes Heart and Whit. This takes shock and bliss and there are still miles to cover. To reveal my real lover. I am androgyny; love to see you cringe in your conservatism. I came here on the bus with the other life-long immigrants, so I will work until death or what's left on the spirit; glad it is eternal and I am diurnal. This word comes when it wants and it does not have to relate-so stop.

Human Rats in the City of Griffins

Grand city streets
occasionally shed their skin –
scaled, ripped to shreds
human to the core.

The evening creeps in
penetrates our bones,
saturating minds
with dark probabilities.

As blind men –
we're stepped over,
poking carefully with canes
into the rushing obstacles,
as passersby.

Yet, we're who're in a hurry,
pointed edges of heavy bags
cut into us, the nameless
figures in motion.
Boulder-sized backpacks
land on our chests.

Ridiculous to promenade
with head raised high,
savoring people and weather.
Trend at present commands,
"Be a rat, run faster than a roach."

Paradise Lost

Once upon a time, they say,
Paradise existed.
Eve consumed the Macintosh,
or was it Granny Smith…
It must've been unbearably sour,
for we to this day still pucker.

How strange… A viper
chosen to seduce,
enwrapped a woman –
naïve as Eve, with its lies.
In ancient mythology
the curling reptile
stands for a phallic symbol.

If we pretend to be detectives –
we'll find the guilty perpetrator.
It was not Eve, as the mindless
'Barbie doll', born out of
innocent man's proud chest…
For his piercing snake eyes,
his savage poisonous nature –
still lead every woman astray.

We're fed applesauce
every day of our lives,
with tartness of *Adam's,* and
Adam's, and *Adam's* acidic hearts.

All is Not Well, in Spring of 2020

My well-rested soul bathes…
Into freshness of spring it plunges.
Except for crumbs, of disgusting evil
spread out – pecked by crows of misery.

The shocking portrayal of overwhelmed
earth, in angst is swallowed up.
Sharp-clawed, spike tailed creature
derives the pleasure in shredding,
turning the blessed creation into dust.

Skin of my afflictions reaped off
by malice of oncoming terror.
Spring's order – to scrub,
cleanse the pain off.

Opposing the stiffening darkness –
trees irradiate smiles,
the sun swathes buildings and people.
Newborn green leafy tongues
glorify their Gardener.
Boldly unveiled buds swell
under persistent warmth,
air expands, nourished by sunshine.

House Sold

Now the house lived in 47 years, hushed
Dishes, tea sets, crystal, silverware
bubble-packed or divvied up, given
to others. Beds stripped of their linens,
frames dismantled, carted away.
Rugs pulled up from wooden floors
not seen in decades. Curtains
pulled down that hung so long, torn
like a scab ripped open.

Room after room, floor after floor,
each returned to a lifeless box, silenced
now that the inhabitants have moved on.
Ghosts walk these cold hallways now,
looking for something they cannot have,
searching for something they cannot name.
Ghosts where once dining room and living
room laughter used to sound.

Now the front door closed and locked.
Now the house hushes, lulls itself, as if
held down by the memory-weight of years.

Bio Notes As Prose Poem

I was born on a fish farm in Guam,
educated privately on my family's estate
in Collinsport, Maine. Began writing poetry
and fiction dealing mostly with vampirism.
Moved to New York, settled in a garret
studio near Snug Harbor on Staten Island.
My best sellers include: *Mummy Said:*
The Unearthed Poetry Of Tut's Mom—
Aunt Nefertiti; Horny: The Sexy Story
Behind The Cloisters' Unicorn Tapestries;
and Marion Davies: Hollywood's Little
Comic Rosebud. I've published a dozen
collections of poetry including the upcoming
Tournafulla Local from Cattywampus Press.
I collect matchboxes once owned by FDR,
the movies of sisters Joan and Constance
Bennett, and various editions of Yoko Ono's
Grapefruit. I participate in Official Scrabble
Tournaments. Often find myself in deep
conversation with the Greek, Roman and
Egyptian statues at The Met Museum.
Consider myself a good friend of His
Holiness The Dalai Lama and communicate
with him daily via telepathy. Been known
to have 'problems' after eating Fettuccine Alfredo.
See my website for further information.

Open Letter To Merv Griffin

Forget Vanna turning letters in her gowns,
forget Pat schmoozing and selling vowels,
forget Alex and guest hosts with their
Daily Doubles. It's Merv Griffin—
singer, entertainer, talk show host, creator
of these shows—Wheel of Fortune and
Jeopardy—who must be making bags
of money delivered nightly to his mansion.
in the sky.

I say bring Merv back! Put him on
prime time again, let him tell us
the latest gossip from beyond.
How are the Gabors? George Sanders?
Have Merv emcee a show that finally
clears up all our questions. Let him
earn his money conjuring up spirit
guests every night.

We want to hear from the real
Jack the Ripper. Watch the Salem
Girls tell all. We want a gab session
with Lizzie Borden and her parents.
Bring Captain Smith back from
the Titanic. Bring Bruno Hauptmann
back, and Baby Lindbergh, and Rasputin,
and that enigma Anastasia.

Merv, think of the extra cash!
Merv, start broadcasting now!

INFORMATION – In this movie

In this movie they talk a lot. But their words get confused. They say "rabbit" when they mean "machine" and "compass" when they mean "daffodil." They say the man is "running" when he is really playing with himself, and that his coat is "purple" when it is really "burning." If he asks to be spanked he is really searching for a definition. His explanation for the door is always the sunrise. He thinks she is listening but she never is.

INFORMATION

She said she was going out the back door, but there was no back door. They listened as the horizon approached, before it wrapped around her like a scarf. They were part of the old story that she hadn't thought of yet, part of the whisper she could never decipher. Her wound was only a color that had been applied incorrectly, her hands a kind of key she thought she had lost.

INFORMATION

The poem never ambitious enough to be included in their discussions, to be included in their anthologies, to be included in the dreams of the co-eds and cheerleaders. Their poems what was left after they walked into the sea, what was left after they described the night, what was left after their fantasy was no longer a fantasy. It was a poem more suitable for writing on a wall, or for setting adrift in a bottle on an angry sea.

heart strings

all
boys
cry,
damp
eyes
faulting
grazed
heart's
injury,
justifying
kisses
lent;
men
never
openly,
pride
quells
rivulets,
sob-strings
tremulous
until
violent
wails;
x-fold
y-chromosomes
zithering . . .

Crossing the River

Spanning the Yangtze River in Nanjing, China, is a legendary bridge — a million and a half tons of concrete and steel, four miles long, with four lanes of vehicular traffic on the upper deck and twin railroad tracks on its lower — where each day the hapless, downtrodden, and depressed come to end their lives.

a bridge crisscrossed
delivers egress –
final goodbyes, hellos intersect –
Janus-like,
keening laudably;
motorists navigate,
oblivious;
precious quivers
release,
swan-dive,
twist
under
viaduct's
whirling x-brace;
Yamahas
zooming.

Aperture's Black Hole

After Rear Window *(Hitchcock, 1954)*

Ambient
Blowup:
Cameraman's
Dark-clothed
Eyepiece
Freeze-Frames
Golden
Hour
Interiors,
Journaling
Kissy- &
Loud-mouthed
Married
Neighbors,
Oculus
Panning,
Questioning
Rear-window
Sfumato
Tableaux;
Umpteen
Viewfinders
Widening
X-times,
Y'all
Zoom in.

Not War

I sit early on to tap the day
and loose my eyes into the thinning sumac leaves
against the grays, brick and sky.
Tapered leaves move in the wind like fingers
on my lower back, the best
argument for letting go,
for coaxing out time's syrup
and turning it to water, ready to run
or to rock in place
or joust with air
as the remaining day requires.

Youth

To have been taken in,
altered
like a dress
with silent, flattening
stitches,
just a few a day,
your very fabric,
your hand
stiffening
and in retreat.

Then threadbare
to have taken in a
child,
a frowning child,
and raised her.

I raised her low
and raised her high,
seeking songs
in a needle's eye.

In the Bud

There was a time
when I could rhyme
but not in this life,
with a knife at my neck.

That's the story
I tell myself,
the roar of it
a kind of hell.

But there's still time --
for the wrinkles of your neck
to be set a-trembling
by a world-embracing throat.

Creation

(or, The Seamstress)

Her stiches are so straight, putting
together different shapes she'll
make a whole and useful garment.
Perfect fitting symmetry created.

There's not one misdirected thread,
for she'll sit patient, and will undo
with just as much enthusiasm.
Her hands will create a dress, a suit,

a skirt that could compete. For her home
she will make a bedspread, a table
cloth and curtains with much care, designed
as if purchased in any fine

city store. She's made for the Christmas
tree out of pieces of felt, fabric
with glitter, sequins and other things,
colorful ornaments, silver

and gold nicely enhanced, everything
as perfect as—her nose? God now
holds those creative hands. Somewhere
in space there is a perfect spot.

Dancing Toward Granada

(From a Dream)

A procession of music and dance has entered
a magnificent hall. The main male and female
dancer in a small sleigh with ropes are pulled along.
They move—one arm forward, hands almost touch,

among other performers who are dancing on
to beautiful music. The full lyrics of the song
which was sung I can't recollect, only these words
in a tenor's voice "… and we'll dance to Granada."

As performers made their exit in full regalia
nearby where I stood, I can't recall if I'd been asked,
but dance instructor to the end, remember shouting
at them, "You could've used more expressive hand

motions as you moved along." And when I awoke,
I could still hear the music, remember the dance,
and a few words to a tune much hauntingly strange
that I'd never heard ". . . and we'll dance to Granada."

Her Story

I wondered what had become of the sweet
And fragrant words she wrote. She didn't paint
Though I tried to move her to observe, greet
And interpret the sunrise, and acquaint
Herself again with her old art; to make
Of remnants pretty flowers. In the dance,
She wished to partner no one. Not to take time
Out for curiosity became her stance.
She only harbored cheerless memories
That seemed to find solace in her mind.
And from her came fewer gentle reveries.
I tried reminding her of beautiful things,

But soon I feared for myself. And always note,
And insist the world remain my open book.

Brooklyn Botanical Garden

For Madeline

One day I'll look at these photographs
yellow narcissus and pink Japanese cherry

see our smiling faces
I'll forget how drained & tense I was

I'll remember the day
woman writers bonded as they marveled

the delicate white flowers
of the paperbush

Local News

He was arrested by the FBI for weapons possession.
A self-proclaimed Proud Boy,
he's had previous run-ins with the law.

His home's an armory of
semi-automatics, Glocks, and a few rapid-fire.
He lives a heartbeat from a school.

He lives a pulse from my home.
Why does he need an arsenal of firearms?
Weapons of war, guns that kill.

I know there are many staunch Trumpers nearby:
rich people, greedy businessmen, Little League coaches.
How many more houses are stockpiled with ammunition?

The husband of a friend belongs to a gun club.
He goes shootin' every Saturday with the boys.
Trumpers and stumpers crashing into bumpers.

Trump's end is near and they're going to war.

A holy war
a war of prejudice
a war within themselves
killing peace.

The World is on Lockdown
We are Sheltering in Place

Grandma Bridie is now 90.
She lives alone baking Irish soda bread
and chocolate chip cookies.
Before the virus, we shopped in supermarkets.
We gathered together without fear.

Now we are told to stay home,
but when you live alone
especially in your senior years
isolation becomes an ugly monster.

Without technology:
no Facebook
no Instagram or TikTok to view
no Zoom conferencing to connect you,

the isolation monster feeds on loneliness
crawling out from the news on TV.
He begins to gnaw at Grandma.

The family that comforts her
is told to avoid her.
She finds it hard to understand, why?

A frightened child calls out in the night
I'm out in the rain where are you?

German Interlude

The TV broadcasts limbo.
I finish my rum-and-coke.

A haze in the room, hot.
She sprinkles cologne about
In a futile gesture—it's
Old, rank, overripe.

We will fly to Germany
And visit cathedrals
And try to forget this summer
In New York City.

Monologue

For a moment our bodies match
As you crawl over me
To lower the air-conditioner.
Your breasts disturb the sweat
Already drying on my stomach.

You tell me about your children
Growing up in Canada
And I feel you slowly draw away
Until you're talking
Only to yourself.

Late Afternoon

Our kid plays in the yard
Poking at things with his stick.

He discovers that the car
Parked in the driveway
Is unlocked—
He climbs inside
And takes a nap.

You hold me so tight
I can hardly breathe.

Chorale

The tender shoot is beautiful.
rising by the hour
in sun and rain, dutiful,
ingesting sunlight's power.

Flowers, opening yet to come
and, oh, the wilting too.
Seeds flying. Roots to become.
Shoots rise anew.

Mushrooms hug decay in gloom.
Wildflowers spread far and wide.
In creation there is room
for transpiring side by side.

The dying and the living plant
twine in one celestial chant.

Reunion

My own life buried deep within
myself before I'm ever dead,
I can't recall what wit or whim
propelled me in the life I led

why I did this, rejected that,
or even how I really looked
aside from snapshots, pasted flat
or hallway portraits, framed and hooked

and what I felt and how I loved
and who I thought I might become
and how in fatal steps I moved
from loss to freedom, to and from…

Except if you, who knew me when,
unearth those former selves again.

Pair

You tramp through the woods and find truffles.
I tramp through the world and find words.
What a pair, escaping troubles,
venturing, glad, undisturbed.

I'll write a poem for you to keep.
It bares my heart and brims with joy
to bring you pleasure while you sleep
and seed your dreams – a clever ploy.

Now let's clean and eat those truffles.
Feast and wash them down with wine
'til gravediggers with their shovels
make our beds for all time.

On the Same Page

two obituaries, New York Times 3/12/2021

1.
A photo shows him hero
of the seas plying the tides
to conquer the Atlantic
in a kayak always keen
for the horizon
finally closing his eyes
on the peak of Kilimanjaro
a happy man, as he said,
he didn't want to die in bed.

2.
Indictments rage his book,
survivor of a death march
who testified how they tried
to camouflage the ovens
smoke forever darkening
his eyes, yet now it seems
one could wake from night
even plan ahead,
even hope to die in bed.

April

In moccasins of deer skin
I walk in beauty
birdsong surfing on a morning breeze
beauty before me
kids in a court slam-dunking the ball
beauty behind me
an orange on a bench left by a homeless man
beauty above me
matriarchal trees nursing buds in their boughs
beauty below me
tiny green tips opening like hungry breaks
beauty all around me
my throat a flute
a troubadour
tootling for my life

**Walk in Beauty,* prayer from The Navajo People

The Grasshoppers and the Ants

a modern foible

In the temple
imagined angels
bestow *bubby* kisses
on their *yarmulkes*
as the pious dance
holding hands
in black ancestral
robes of mystic seers
kibitz holy books
to join the hoopla---
see spines unwind from bindings
letters vining *horas* across floors
bearded *Talmuds* twirl-debating laws

In the kitchens
sheiteled wives
prepare for sabbath
braiding *challah*
boiling chicken
washing ironing
setting table
sweeping dusting
mending tending babies
lighting candles
offering the sabbath prayer
bearing earfuls of the husband's
daily blessing----
not born a woman
thank you God.

Aspiration

Vaguely
my mind roams
looking for one, but
finds no poem in me—
nothing lodged
that needs emergence,
no surge
of prosodic current. Not
even a twinge.
What if…
I just adjust
to the ordinary surround.
In other words, note
whatever is
and loosen the bind by
minding
the content of now.
.

Out of Doors

these days, when
it's temperate
I choose to walk
on the sunny side—
being
that I consider
our local star
my friend…
beaming down
light and warmth
on me
at precisely
the right distance
for healing
and regeneration.

Roth

A bad back
demands he stand
erect
at his desk, where
driven, he writes
prodigious—
as if sweating
the rich panoply
of words
out his pores.

Characters and
situations in his prose
are mined
in pithy, elemental
detail;
the comedic timing
is perfect.

Compelled
I turn page after page
rapt
in the briny, fulsome
read of his book.

When I was 17…

my boyfriend told me
he wanted me to be his wife.
It sounded romantic at first.
He said two will become one.
I thought that would make me
a half. I didn't want to be a half.
I hadn't yet become whole.

When Biden Was Announced The Winner…

Did you whistle and shout
Do the hokey pokey
And shake it all about?
Did you bang pots
Dance hip hop
Tap, jazz, ballet
Do the Nae Nae?
Did you yell *"WOOHOO!"*
Did you do the boogaloo
Do-si-do & skip to my Lou?
Or did you simply sigh "Whewww!"?

Not Even In My Dreams

(for an ex)

I dreamt I tried to give him back
A piece of him
Tried to explain
His mind was splitting
But just as in waking life
All my love could not
Put his mind back together again

Hi Ol silver away Or easythere

big fella   Those precious bullets fit perfect
in his gun chamber   A point blank directive like
the great horse between his legs   Hinted criminal
and masked mannish   The bizarre hero   Breaker of
rules with his Indian/love pets that calico pony girlish
Scout   The boys get off alone as they ever return to the
wild where even Rossini joins them   A galloping phallus
crescendo after crescendo they frolic together then save
the world for the bourgeoisie   Cover their tracks straight
though not < Tonto love Keemosabe >

<Ranger is thrilled when you tickle his handgun that
shoots shoots shoots Hi OL Silver I'm gay   With

my silk sash and just Tonto sees my naked self as i
gallop into his tumbleweed   We ramble and horse
around up the earthy trail   HI OL Silver I'm gay >

You and I even at seventy seven don't

understand the meaningless heavens no no
we're too unconscious in chairs near
table the best we can swing
is a dance in a fable

Pass outdoor restaurants where dusty
leaves barely visible fall sadly
to the ground

This closing darkness is absurd   It's
a hi goodbye with barely a word

Know each time we meet we kiss de/feet

Into museums the cultured go talking
of Rembrandt & Vincent Van Gogh Their
walking there helps fiddles to fiddle
right in the middle   right
in the middle

after "The Love Song of J Alfred Prufrock" T.S. Eliot

d
l i
i n
u g
B u i l d i n g s
p r e s s from s k i e s
t o n s o f s t r e s s
in c o n c e n t r a t e d
s t r e n g t h .

H e a r t e d m i n d s
p u t t h e m t h e r e
needing s t a b i l i t y

E a c h d a y t h e s e
m o n u m e n t s
c e l e br a t e u s
i n c o n c r e t e
s e c u r i t y .

W e o w n a w a l l.
F e e l a d o o r.
Ceiling o u r s e l v e s
f r o m t h e s k y
Possessing a deep black hole
with knob and lock to funnel in or tunnel out.
We've constructed t o g e t h e r a cemented universe

Loud
and
loquacious,
the lone bird
calls out —
long before
the sky
illuminates.

Watchful
and
lethargic,
the lone writer
peers out —
slowly emerging
from the
gossamered mantle.

Muddled
and
on the move,
long walks settle —
resolutions become
clear.

Hushed
and
pensive,
making headway —
regaining ground.

Darkness as Light

Finding
that darkness,
spurred a
delve into
the deep —

bulbs, roots,
worms, seeds,
stones, rocks,
boulders —

boulders that peek
aboveground,
akin to icebergs,
revealed for all
to see — partly.

I
replaced
darkness
with light.

Sodden

Quivering,
pansy petals
empty themselves
of collected
rainwater.

Strengthening,
stems reach
for the first
rays of sun
in a week.

Emboldened,
buds pop,
twirling
multi-colored
pinwheels.

Astonished,
we sit back
to watch.

How could I not?

She pussy-foots around trying not to disturb me.
But when she does the consequences are enormous
for her for me and for the pigeons in Central Park
who listen to these two very old women
squabble writhe torture suffer.
One never letting on the other broadcasting it all
on this small town broadsheet I call a poem.

Not even allowed to kiss (Covid)
the other so afraid of germs and people
of life itself but she loves to kiss
and to love too   she loves to
and me she loves me so she says "I love you" often
This leaves me flummoxed and discombobulated.
I love her. But listening to her enthuse over the I Ching,
WBAI Conspiracy Theories Astrology and The Man Upstairs.
That's when the torture of bedding down with
this Really Good Girl begins.

She flies with the pinkest angels.
Feeds sick pigeons who roost in her air shaft.
Her mice are all safe and well fed in Have-A-Heart Mousetraps.
She caught one once and released it in the lobby
of her tenement in Alphabet city.
"Too cold to put him on the street."
I visited her room for the first fifteen years. No More.

A Mad Woman's Nest. A Fairy's Aerie.

Oh poor things, can't see or hear much anymore.
We have our dignity (not easy with me around).
Oh poor poor suffering humanity.
How could I not love such an old true friend?

A GUY ONCE ASKED ME HOW IMPORTANT IS IT FOR A WOMAN TO COME?

I said, "How important is it for you to come?"

If somewhere a clitorectomy is done
It's done to me. I'm never free. My feet
are bound. I early learned to make no sound.

Choreographed a dance I performed in silence.
Rocked and rocked in place 'til the curtain fell.
About not being able to speak. Living in Hell.

A dance about how I couldn't know what I knew.
Because I didn't know? Stupid? Scared?
Rocked and rocked and didn't know why.
Was there applause? Couldn't hear it.
Couldn't know because
I had to be that stupid.

They used to say
"men never make passes at girls:
With fat asses
Bad Faces
Who wear glasses
Who prefer lasses
Who are conscious"

Second dose

Monday

I am hungry for classical music. Like a snake,
I sidewind closer & closer, stepping numerous times
in time, 6 ft. apart, lane by lane where games used to play.
All military is now represented in camouflage,
all the soldiers are young & cute. I'm not dead yet—
I want to strike & not get any sicker.
I don't like being too tired. Will I sleep this time around?
Will I keep my food down? (Pause for H2O sipping).
Is it raining outside? Will my love freak out tomorrow?
(It's his first time). Are we all becoming snakes?
Clair de lune is playing. My favorite—I wish I could
swallow this moon auditory treat whole,
& digest it for weeks.

Wednesday

Low-grade fever is now gone. I woke up to red rashes
from my forehead to my chest. Dr. on the videophone
doesn't think it's because of the vaccination.
"Did you eat or wear anything unusual?" he asked me.
I don't remember. I'm really feeling itchy—am I
shedding my old skin away? Did I eat the wrong rat?
Benadryl's now hitting my brain—
Damn—my blood's now tasting the antihistamines.
Damn—fell asleep for an hour—Hubby's on the phone
talking to lawyers (he's a lawyer; no worries, he's working).
Can't roam yet. I hear violin & piano music across the street.
Still hungry—for cake & classical music.

Mud Season

It’s still not safe to walk into the woods,
the neighborhood online streaming news warned
the river inhabitants. The walking paths are filled with water.

If you walk it now, the path will expand
& it will eventually wash away.

Animals are hiding in the branches, rustling & chattering
as the rain drips from the oak trees.

Please wear waders, we were warned:
Stay away from the river.

Leave the mud in the mud room—
it’ll go everywhere.

“Don’t worry, the rain will stop soon.
We will explore the forest again
when the mud is done running free.”

“When will that be?” I wondered aloud,
when Dad started a fire in the fireplace.

“It’s still April, heavy & wet,
thick into mud season.”
The earth is no longer frozen—

“The month is still soft like the ground.
We have to be patient now,
so that good things can come forth.”

Shallow

Gaining your acceptance
was not an easy shimmer.

As the drops fell from Heaven,
reflections radiated the river

& I tried to find your face
on the other side of the mirror,

but the deepness
I've been searching for,
was way too shallow.

Your version of love
only works with cocktails.

& the glitter gained
doesn't always turn into gold,

& I'm drinking cold gin,
wondering what could have been

but it was too hollow;
the river's too shallow.

The Last Clippity Went Clop (from June Came Easy)

These boots knew better
than to walk me down these old familiar streets
these feet walked me down
these eyes lost in some search for transcendence
this pen silent witness / obedient scribe
this willful hand doodles on napkins…scraps of any blank paper
this hand with a life of its own
feels a conundrum
when the beat comes undone
un-drum
no rhythm
no spring in the step
no steps
no cause
no applause
well, the die is not yet cast nor is the cast at hand
pen in hand / the page waits

quiet house
at last some thoughts can be heard above the ringing of the phones
the phoning of friends, worries, stories, complaints, plans…
suspicions of hormones, neurons, synapses, being responsible
for all that…wives' tales and myths about virgins and
Virgil's footsteps on the path
arrested by blossoms…cherry magnolia dogwood
kneeling at the cups of tulips true and truly
these boots now off
these feet now bare

Free Range Thinker

Free range thinker
available to tinker
but not with a bell
while we cast us this spell…

Free range thinker
sometime drinker
never a stinker!

Free range thinker
arrested, ass in the clinker
rose colored glasses now pinker!

Free range think
er…I spy you and wink
so you're back now from the brink
swim! swim! swim! don't sink!

Free range thinker
tattooed body inker
colored drawings head to toe
he's always at it, don't you know?

Salt Lick

Can I take the salt out of my wounds?
it was rubbed in so deep
marinating me in a hot peppery sauce
bottled up
waiting   to   pop my cork

I lick and lick and lick and lick
I took "a licking and kept on ticking"
ticking with salt in my wounds

There was scar tissue
someone said "scar tissue never heals"
scar tissue some where in the middle of two veins
or an artery and a vein (pulmonary plumbing evades me)
somewhere in the middle of two veins
or an artery and a vein
or a parent not quite sane
or your brother's name is Cain
some where one day there's a healing
some Gorilla Glue action
some deep down traction
in the cellular level
in the cellar
there's a healing
from the salt of the earth
on the tongue
salt
lick!

Thoughts

don’t seem to want to sing to me
My heart does not want to dance for me
Yet happy I am without romance
with the warmth of the sun a
feline companion generous family
and great long-time friends!

Colors

Blues can soften the mood
or push one over the edge

Reds charge on like fire to
empower emotions

Yellows brighten the day
to dry out the rain

Oranges escape darkness
making dead leaves glisten

Greens awaken the path
that leads to the future

What's Lost in Being Here

I woke to know the unanswerable.
At last I knew
I knew it all. Something pulled at me. The evening opened up.

From those who say they know for sure, I'd already learned
fixed thoughts hang out on broken limbs.
And science… is evolution all there is?

The answer is purest absolute.
There's nothing lost in being here. Except
that wonder when you wake to know you know it all.

In Bed She Reads Me the Obituaries

"The only way to live is to forget you are going to die."
        Somerset Maugham

In bed I listen to her itemize the litany of finality:
        one man's heart stroke,
        a woman pregnant dead at birth,
notices on organs black as smoke.

She hugs me, glad the present's what we share.
        "We're here," she laughs too loud. I sigh
"We should be terrified." She chides me
for dark thoughts; guffaws, "We got this far!"

The night still rings toward rang, an end to first-
hand amusement. Nonetheless
touch recalled from yesterday still jolts regret,
when nothing's next.

The Praying Mantis

The praying mantis
an icon on my computer screen
her arms tai-chi ready. She senses I am eager,
erect with my need to spill seed, to enter
her predaceous beauty, her with the heart-shaped face,
the black spot on her spread-wing tail.

Creation schools me to be devoured.
To accept the crunch, crackle, pop,
the inside scream so loud none can hear it.

I know this is the moment, and I am ready.
Her arms pray for me to enter,
ready for me to plant my continuity into her body,
assuaging her hunger, satisfying my own.

The Nursing Home

Know them by the memories they keep,
Muttering to imaginary friends,
Their close-by hand-holding Minders.

Memories sit with them at breakfast or
At afternoon coffee and sweet cakes,
Keeping them company.

Speak to the ones who flutter with
Firefly butterflies before they
Fly away, never to come back.

What comes to us in nightmares comes
To them elegiacally, from
Mildly mildewed moth ball closets.

Happy memories crowd out their
Present, help propel them toward,
Yes, they-know-it's-coming end.

In denial and why not?
Memories are better than dreams.
No one wants to die alone.

Red-Lacquered Hooves

Her sleigh cruises earth-low, enough
for me to climb aboard to a
Lovely view. She is cuddled in
Baby pink bunting. I wear white.

Reindeer hooves begin to climb
Before long, prancing into
Sparse-air, rarefied oxygen
Only she and orchids inhale.

I can't breathe her air. I jump.
Land, as usual, banged-up,
Weighed down by a broken heart,
The heart that breaks each jump.

Landward I gaze sleigh-ward, my
Eyes rise highest to higher
Than I could ever ever go.
Destiny takes her where she must.

Red lacquered hooves never stop
Dancing on. Cruel masters
Compel her to climb, to dive,
To circle the planet each year.

She, sleeping, is their one parcel,
Wrapped in motherly blankets and bows,
While I, small, smaller, smallest, disappear,
Keening for her to come home.

What Poets Do in a Pandemic

Poets lay waste to your self-lies,
Hurl you backward, puzzled and stunned.
Gasping for air, you look upward

To see only awkward angles,
Ruminations, people fueled by
Ego, living in surround-sound.

Blinking in dazed disbelief,
You see you are one of them.

Poets abruptly kidnap you,
Plucking you out of the mundane
To a sight that, at first, blinds you.

Blazing vistas are too
Beautiful to endure.

Like a moth, you cease to
Fear death.

Soothed, you invite the
Engulfing madness.

Dodging to the Election

The moderator did
not ask again
the question
he asked the candidate
who instead answered a question
not asked.

Then on to the next
question. A question whose deflection
against it was born
before
the question itself
came into being.

Modern Man

The core of him –
dense with weary,

an invisible weight,

pulls him to
unforeseen places.

Places to navigate with
no paradigms to wrap
around him.

No beacon to beckon a truth.

A place where words are dances
between significances.

Phantasm of the Library

Gaunt –

covered by a membrane
of translucent blue skin,

long grey hair,
strands wound around
each other like snakes writhing in the wild.

She prowls aisle to aisle
silent on bare feet
bleached like a corpse.

Footprints vaporize in an instant.

Skeletal hands clutch
carefully chosen books.

She studies each
page. Feels each word
with the tips of her boney fingers

as she carries them
to her side of time.

Telling the Story

Dear Friend,
Good to finally see each other
in real time. Socially distanced
on a park bench, masks giving
a semblance of safety and
equity as we sit in attendance
thru our eyes.

Our eyes. They carry the
stuffed emotions overflowing
our hearts. We talk. Compare
notes. We talk more. It's easy
breezy conversation. Silently I
command: I need you to READ
MY EYES!

I'm willing the upper half of my
face to telegraph the truth of my
fears. To tell you what I dreamt
last night. The words stick in my
throat. The admission voiceless.
I take a breath. Can you see how
afraid I am of getting sick?

Leaving the City

So here's the truth …

I am so not comfortable living in
nature, in the country and although
I love reading Mary Oliver's poetry,
on any summer day I'm still not
eager to make friends with wild
turkeys and deer, coupled with no
respite from "I'm soaking-wet-in-
this-unbearably-hot-sun" with
insects magnetically adhering to the
seen and unseen parts of me or later,
when it's night and nothing, I mean
absolutely nothing is visible outside
the window and it's quiet, oh so
terribly quiet the silence deafening,
well I just want to run shrieking back
to the city leaving a note for my friends
that hey, I love you guys, I really do,
but I'm just not, repeat, I'm just not
… a country kind of gal.

What Price?

O, the tangled webs we script;
their content bringing fear.
Stark truth rears its homely head;
we tremble at the sight of our creation….

Writing is of the mind
but not purely.
It can prompt a visceral response –
deep feelings apart from the cerebral,
like *angst* prompted by the seed of an idea
that strikes a dissonant chord; crosses a bridge
to a physical feeling of dread.

What price this self-inflicted joy of expression
brought about by stints of pen-to-page?
Other than carpel tunnel/curvature of spine/eye strain/
stiff neck/aching shoulders and back/discomfort of
sleep deprivation caused by deadlines to be met
or some stream-of-consciousness marathon run amok,
what price?

Writing is of the mind.

Fate: Seven Senryu

A name, dates: *Born — Died*
quiet stone stoic displays
on its face, a life.

Finite time on Earth.
Shame when a mature man knows
not which road to take.

Quagmires, mazes…
surefooted are mountain goats.
Wish I knew my path.

Life giver-taker,
gaseous ball of wax and wane
does not rise or set.

Sun not a solid
though staid each day Earth rotates.
Merrily we roll.

Pray this orbit holds
lest we freeze or burn to death.
Things we can't control.

Happy thought: *we're here;*
alive to ask what awaits.
Raise a glass to fate.

A Verse Duet

Poetry Frame of Mind

Many poets are tortured souls, driven to drugs,
drink, suicide…driven to write.
Abused as children; racked by ailment,
witnesses to atrocities of war, domestic strife,
unable to deal with love unrequited,
ones who would take an innocent life —
give thanks to the muse that sits in attendance,
the pen that waits for inspiration, that prize
often the confluence of heaven/hell articulated.
Rejoice, the poet's soul is saved!
Sanity, or *insanity*, suspended for a time.

Of all the many therapies, for me it's poetry.
Music, equestrian, axe-throwing sessions
to relieve tension, of all the healing roads to take,
I choose to face the page.
No pain but for catharsis when images are loosed —
one's naked self confronted in verse.
Whatever the throes, I'd rather give birth to a poem.

On Feeling the Futility of Words

All the words I ever wrote/with pleasure those yet to write
hoping to bring joy, peace (war could be incited), reverie
for nature's panoply, this poetry so dear I'll concede.
Quiet my instrument forever; weep then smile, emerging
from a bloody battle won if this be the way, if ever the need,
to save the lives of my beloved daughter and son.

Salutations

November 2020

Orange leaves as confetti celebrate the streets while a white
Guy in shorts celebrates global warming, balmy November.
Masked tenants sit on stoops.

I'm on my way to Foodtown, ready to stock up for the viral
Second wave, while enjoying the gentle breeze, quiet streets.
The city festooned with plywood and colored light bulbs for
Outdoor dining resembling succahs at Tishrei's Haifa hotels.
I wish you saw this.

You stay in your home, Kate, safe upstate,
Percolating pregnancy, pacing your fancy-shmancy floors.

Greetings from NYC
From your cheap aunt
The one with the bad gifts. The Hospital Worker.
Our Lady of Angry Outbursts.
I sell hello with a drink in my hand.

Blessings on your husband's new Lexus.

Joe

He turns his sunburned, Nordic face.
Stares at dancers pecan-colored,
Walnut-colored;
Some the colors of various legumes.
He covets their sun-resistant melanin,
Envies such protection.

He bites his sandwich.

Around him, the park brims laughter, screams,
The wheels of double seat strollers
Squeaking on asphalt.
The sun blesses the trees;
Heat on shrubs, tufts of grass, dried moss
Climbing a fence embracing light.

Another bite of roast beef.

The thirsty man envisions fjords – glinting streams –
White specks on rocks, cool water.

He crumples his paper bag,
Throws it out, dirty napkin inside.
He is a seed in the sliced, Big Apple.
Only the park cameras notice.

From the Hallway Closet

She stole grandma's mink.
Well, actually it was squirrel.
Grandpa was poor.

My cousin, age eighteen.
The DNA of grandpa's Belarus bride,
Coursing through her veins.

It is shiva…

My mom and aunt eat *baklava* and coffee.
Grandpa is crying.
The world has changed, I know this
And I am a child.

Sheila the thief confronts me near the bathroom.
Tells me about the fur she took like cash owed
From a family that did not love her.
A debt, she says: "long overdue".

Ephemeral

So ephemeral is springtime!
One day, tree branches are swathed in blossoms.
The next day, petals are falling heavily—
tears shed by mourners at a gravesite.

Like loved ones,
trees have not perished—
Both transformed,
unrecognizable.

Dental Dismay

Our dentists we will in more than one-way pay,
to hell with pride, we want to run and hide,
reminder cards from dentists cause dismay.

I'm frightened by the thought of tooth decay,
and killer drills which work their wiles inside,
("Now, open wide!")
our dentists we will in more than one way pay.

Sly spinning metal twists and shouts and, "Hey!
my blankin' gums are really getting fried!"
Reminder cards from dentists cause dismay;

And root canals are not my friends—no way!
when nerves are carved my head goes for a ride....
our dentists we will in more than one-way pay.

"You *MUST* go see a dentist", screamed Fay Wray;
when King Kong got the bill he nearly died!
Reminder cards from dentists cause dismay!

I'm at a floss for words, though this I'll say:
"I'd rather let *my* next appointment slide!"
Our dentists we will in more than one-way pay,
reminder cards from dentists cause dismay.

Sting

It probably knew the outcome
on some level,
zipping like a meteorite
between lowered glass
and the car door frame

a hovering flying saucer
waiting for the right time

Attack!
at my face
swipe, swipe, careen
CRASH!
God damn it!

This morning, in North Valley Stream
a bee came at me,
my car smashed in like the faces
of Ali and Frasier
in "The Thriller in Manila"

the pole I hit, like the bee,
unscathed

Old But Not Useless

She raged for weeks,
angry, wrathful, stubborn

A few months earlier,
when old age had taken over,
I had hoped to appease her crankiness
by treating her to a dismantling

Nearly a few grand later,
though somewhat raspy,
she now never misses when I turn her on
I've decided to hold onto the old gal

My car, dented and damaged,
ancient as a forgotten compost heap,
missing two of her front lenses,
still delivers

Turned a corner

I have turned a corner of a circle
massive thoughts like hurricanes
no longer rule
feelings coming at me
from elsewhere and beyond
I will not fail
When silence falls slowly
rolling in like Juno snow
covering crisp sharpness
blankets on my cries
I shuffle the cards
Gratitude comes up and grace
the world is calling me
for change
for silence
for – give – ness
for gratitude
another corner of a circle to be turned

Surfacing

Amazed at all I know already
surprised at my readiness
my love for me was buried deep
alive but almost not
struggling to splatter out
cracking my shell like a croc
out of my egg starving
surfacing shaking
for everyone who sees

Dr. Ignaz Semmelweis: 1818 – 1865

"The Savior of Mothers"

He screamed the halls
begging their cadaver-drenched hands meet water;
his peers mocking and scornful,
ignoring his pleas,
palpable frustration,
mothers – his only validation.

While his patients lived to hold
the newborns from their wombs,
the other doctors turned, blind-eyed,
while their patients died and died,
as those doctors went from morgue to pre-natal,
contamination-by-proxy.

176 years ahead of his time,
they listened too late,
sealing the fate
of so many mothers,
while Dr. Semmelweis was forced to endure
and witness their ignorance;
powerless, heart-broken, defeated,
as he watched dreams die.

His words echo through time,
what might he now ask?
"So simple a task,
to just wear a mask"?

I Did

for my Martin
8.1.20

Fifty years ago today, my heart leapt.
My biggest worries were:
Is my veil poufy enough?
Too poufy?
Not to drop wine
on the lovely white lace.

We had to wait till sundown,
it was a Saturday evening,
my grandmother, Matron-of-Honor.
Afraid I'd faint,
my grandfather promised to stand behind me
to hold me up.
I felt his hand on my back, reassured.

Family around me, friends behind,
the Rabbi began.
I said, "I do."
The Rabbi said,
"I'm glad you do, but I haven't asked you yet."
Comic relief.

We continued our vows.
The Rabbi before us,
you by my side,
I needed nothing more.
Everything was right with the world.
I do. I did. I would again.
And again and again.

Only I

Only I remember
when we led a thousand lives
and filled a thousand dreams.

Only I remember
when you were young and strong
when we pushed away old age
and chased a thousand stars.

Only I remember
when your shock of hair was brown
and your smile drew a crescent moon.

Only I remember
from fountains of before
when our passion flew like soaring birds
no one could ask for more.

Only I remember
when left with what they cannot see
memories we shared forever…
you and me.

If time removes my being,
if I'm not left to see,
who will carry our memories,
who then if not but me?

Only I remember
now a solo flight,
which rides along the sunset,
and spills into the night.

First Born

Center of the universe
How could I have known
there would be others?

When my parents hugged,
I was the pastrami between the rye
the marshmallow inside the Twinkie.

My grandparents adored me.
The first grandchild, female
the daughter they never had.

I was given cultured pearls
a fake mink stole
and my own fishing rod.

When I turned three, Linda,
my mother's little sister,
came to live with us.

One night I stayed with my *bubbie*
a Russian woman in her 90s
who badmouthed my aunt.

"Stop saying bad things about Linda
or I won't come back."
She stopped.

The power of the first born.

Don't Sit Next to Me

Some days I forget
I walk out without my mask
Pale blue disposables take
me by surprise

Is this real?
Remember the days of
small jampacked tables
at Cornelia Street Café?

I loved the crowds of New York City
restaurants, cafes, book stores,
the subway. *Crowded*
has taken on a new meaning

Anxious when the subway doors open
I used to read, now
scrutinize everyone
Don't sit next to me.

No mask
I move to another seat or car
Too crowded
I wait for the next train

When I arrive at my destination
I remove my pale blue disposable
wash my hands
and take a deep breath.

"I'm Gay"

I leapt beyond the edge
of the one-hundred-foot drop into the river.
My elbow-locked arms spread wide,
a perfect swan dive,
hands trembling from fear of crashing into a foot
of rocky water overridden
by powerful hopes of landing smoothly
in the deep pool; I straightened my body,
plunging head first.
Seated with you both in your den
where the family lolls about
all day, relaxing, watching TV.
Now late evening, the TV off,
and I have said to you
those dreaded words—
I hit the water, my fists and arms
penetrating the surface. Hurtling deep
into the pool never touching bottom,
the water ice cold,
fed by an underground spring.

What Stories Do Pictures Tell?

I'd always wanted one
Now I have it   An MRI
Of my brain   I used to fantasize
It would be of great scientific interest—
I would be such a famous memoirist
recounting tales of New Testament visions
But I never wrote my life story
Now I just want to know if it
Delivers the data on why I have been
Leaving the burner on the stove
Still lit after my omelet is done
and why I left the front door
Open when I took the train into the city
They posted the radiologist's report
online, the only two familiar words,
"infarct" and "ischemia" don't sound so good to me
I meet with my neurologist next week
Maybe I should ask her if
I should stop fantasizing about dying
in my nineties, healthy and asleep

The Robe

Now everything's gone except his robe.
My mother wanted our father's clothing
	out of the closet right away;
	Done.
Some survivors want the clothes to disappear,
	others to leave them undisturbed, as a way of saying,
	"He was *here*. He still *is*. He made a difference."
By chance or by design the robe escaped the emptying.
	Somehow here it remained, hanging—a loose garment of
	terrycloth
	lightly draped over the shoulders of a ghost.
Three days later my mother opened the closet door
	expecting it to be empty but shocked at the sight
	of a near-human form defiantly hanging there before her.
"Daddy's robe!" she blurted out, her face
	ashen with tears welling up
	in anguish over never mending the brokenness.

Made in the USA
Middletown, DE
13 May 2022

65675461R00086